Consciously Creating Circumstances

by

George Winslow Plummer

THE BOOK TREE
San Diego, California

First published
1935

ISBN 978-1-58509-310-6

Cover layout and design
by Toni Villalas

Published by
The Book Tree
P.O. Box 16476
San Diego, CA 92176
www.thebooktree.com

We provide fascinating and educational products to help awaken the public to new ideas and
information that would not be available otherwise.
Call 1 (800) 700-8733 for our *FREE BOOK TREE CATALOG*.

INTRODUCTION

This is a powerful how-to book on improving your mind and body, aligning yourself with nature's harmony, and living a happier and better life. The wisdom employed in these teachings comes from the school of Rosicrucianism, a mystical organization that has been around for centuries. This book will show you how to use the source of your power, achieve desires, use the law of attraction, uplift your basic attitude, improve concentration, control your thoughts, and achieve health and wealth. A highly recommended classic.

Paul Tice

FOREWORD

THIS innocuous-looking little book by George Winslow Plummer is full of metaphysical dynamite capable of effects baleful or beneficient according to what I may call the innate altruism and enlightenment of the person who essays to employ the technique herein set forth. For this particular teaching, though couched in a form capable of being grasped by the average reader, is really a fragment of a most ancient and abstruse Wisdom jealously guarded by its custodians throughout the world and adown the ages on account of its potency for evil when misapplied.

The Rosicrucian Fraternity has ever been, from far back, one of these custodians, and as Dr. Plummer is not only a member of the Society of Rosicrucians, but a leader thereof, I infer that he knows and assumes the responsibilities involved in placing so much power—for knowledge is power—in the hands of any chance reader of the book, regardless of his rectitude. He is probably right in taking this chance, because when the house is on fire one throws all the valuables out of the window, in the hope of saving some of them, regardless of what may become of the rest. Now that this house of all humanity, the world, is so ablaze, he does well to place this knowledge at the disposal of everyone, because the situation can be saved only by such realizations coupled with such a code of action on the part of men of good will, as are here set forth with such precision and clarity. The chance that the teachings of the book may be abused must be taken, therefore.

The precautionary and warning note is sounded, to be sure, by Dr. Plummer in his final chapter, and in such admonitions as "Having satisfied yourself that your predominating desire is worthy, that it involves no harm or detriment to another, and that it will work out to the advantage of others beside yourself," but I had an uncle—and there are many like him—who had no difficulty in satisfying him-self as to all these things when putting through one of his shady—even nefarious—schemes to his own advantage.

Therefore while highly recommending this book to those whose life and character have made them ready to receive its teachings, I am constrained to remind every reader that he who would wield Ex-calibur should have not only the strong arm, but the unselfish and compassionate heart of King Arthur.

—CLAUDE BRAGDON

CONTENTS

9

CHAPTER 1

THE SOURCE OF POWER

IT is evident that the great, successful or happy people of this world have access to some power that obscure, unhappy failures know little or nothing about—"a power which erring men call chance."

Perhaps you think it's just good luck that brings success, and let it go at that. But you miss something very important if you think that.

This is written for those willing to consider the possibility that something other than just luck or heredity bestows happiness on one and failure on another. This book describes a method of attack on the problems of life that thousands of happy people of merely average abilities have successfully employed. Yes, *countless* thousands, even though many of them did not realize what they were using.

If you seek help and are not afflicted with a closed mind, you can use the same power that has served these people. I *can* and *will* tell you about it. We shall start with a few ideas that you and I cannot avoid agreeing on, and then base the rest of our work on what we mutually agree is *so*. Let us, in short, "consider the reason of the case, for nothing is Law that is not reason."

As we look about us in the world our senses inform us that it is full of objects of all sorts: houses, trees, people. We give the general name of "things," or FORMS, to these objects.

Closer inspection informs us that each object has its individual characteristics, such as odor, density, firmness, weight, color, and we find that these objects are made of the same substances in varying physical or chemical combinations. So we say that the objects composing our environment are made of MATTER, and the state in which matter usually appears is VISIBLE.

Now as we look more intently, we observe that there are other conditions in our world that are INVISIBLE. We see the *fall* of an apple to the ground from a tree; the *cause* of the fall remains invisible. Forces of many kinds are evidently in play. We do not see the forces or energies themselves, but they are the CAUSES of all that we do see. What we see are the results—called PHENOMENA, or ACTIONS and STATES OF BEING.

Plants, animals and human bodies change in size, but we do not *see* the energy that makes them increase. We observe people moving about, but we do not see what makes them move about. We think, but we do not see our thoughts. We listen to the radio, send telegrams, speak over the telephone, or push a button for lights in our rooms but we do not see the energy on the way. We see a hen pecking about the poultry yard; in a short time she lays an egg, which in due time becomes a chicken, and later that chicken becomes the full grown bird, reproducing the process of life. A great drama of forces constantly unfolds before us.

So observation teaches us, correctly, that we live not only in a visible world of matter, but also in an invisible world of forces and energies that produce the visible things in our environment.

We recognize these visible forms and we sense the invisible forces behind them through a power we call MIND. No human being has ever seen mind, yet the existence of such a power is the most obvious thing in all our understanding.

Everything in this world about us that *man* has produced began as a thought in the mind of some man. Your home existed in the builder's mind before it took form. Your car took form first in the maker's mind. Everything that we do, individually or collectively, begins first in the THOUGHT OF THE THING. No matter how suddenly we do a thing at times, we THINK OF IT FIRST. Sometimes we act quickly on the thought; sometimes we have to wait until we can develop conditions favorable to its accomplishment.

Also, as we look about us, we observe many forms of matter that were *not* produced by the hand of man, for they express characteristics that no human being has ever produced. Man cannot create a tree, for instance, or an ocean, or a robin. Yet they too must have begun in *a* mind. IN WHAT MIND AND WITH WHAT THOUGHT DID THEY BEGIN?

Before answering the last question, let us look around us some more. We observe that the plant of yesterday is a bit higher today. The little child of last year is larger and abler. We note certain changes in ourselves with the advance of time. We cannot SEE what causes this increase in size, ability, etc., but the fact stares us in the face. Look again, this time at another class of things. That building, begun a few weeks ago, is steadily increasing in size. A railroad has increased its mileage. A bridge is ready for the last span. We CAN see that what makes *them* increase is the hand of man.

So we have before us two different pictures of increase. One springs from the efforts of man, on the visible plane. The other is directed from some invisible plane, and is *not* due to man's efforts. These changes in our environment we call GROWTH. We note that this growth is effected by man in some cases, and by some other power or agency in other cases. But originating in some MIND, *somewhere,* in every case.

Now let us try to discover whether there are *really* two kinds of growth, one caused by man and one caused by something else. There *seem* to be two, but is it truly so?

No sensible person believes that man just happened. He too is a phenomenon, *a fact*, with an invisible cause. We have agreed that this cause can only be man or something other than man. But man did not cause himself: something else brought him into being. Therefore this something else causes not only mountains and oceans, which are beyond man's control, but also causes everything that man *appears* to cause, *because it caused man himself to come into existence*.

Thus we see that there is but ONE BASIC CAUSE of all things that are or ever were. We therefore call it the GREAT FIRST CAUSE. Some call it GOD. Some call it SPIRIT. Whatever term we use, we remember that it operates through MIND, and, since it causes all things, UNIVERSAL MIND. Though some people tie this fact up with a religion or theology, the acceptance of a Universal Mind is imperative from the standpoint of simple logic alone.

ALL POWER COMES FROM ONE SOURCE TODAY, JUST AS IT DID BEFORE THE BEGINNING OF "THINGS."

This great, invisible cause acts through what we term UNIVERSAL MIND—the Intelligence directing all the forces that produced man and through which man, on a much smaller scale, produces the various changes in his environment.

CHAPTER 2

DUAL ACTION

W E agreed at the beginning of this discussion to start with some things so evident that we could easily agree on them.

From there we arrived at an analysis of what was behind those things that we agreed on. We decided that every thing in Nature or Man's World arises from one basic cause, which is invisible, universal, mental, creative, and *not material*, and we called the expression of this great first cause the UNIVERSAL MIND.

What does that mean to us *personally* and *practically?* If, for instance, we should discover that *each* of us can use that fact consciously to our own advantage, wouldn't that be a great discovery? Let us see.

How can we get at least a partial idea of what mind is? I suggest a comparison that has been helpful to many people in gaining a better understanding of this very important point.

On any electric circuit we find different kinds of appliances functioning. Vacuum cleaners, lamps, bells, motors, are all drawing their power to operate from the dynamo in the powerhouse. A lamp draws much less *power* than a big motor uses, but they all operate on the same electrical voltage. Break the circuit to the dynamo; the lamp goes out, the motor slows down to rest, the vacuum cleaner stops whirring, proving that the one source supplies them all.

Mind is something like that. Mind itself is the *source* of power, comparable to the dynamo. Individually we are tied in to that one infinite source, just as the lamps and motors are tied in to the dynamo. And we individually vary a lot in the amount of power we develop from the same voltage, just as the big motor develops much more power than the little motor does. But we are all tied in to that dynamo of limitless power called the Universal Mind.

The development and bettering of your own life depends on your learning how to draw *more power* from that great source, for the beautiful fact is that human machines can *increase* their own power, whereas mechanical contrivances cannot.

So we see that when man *thinks*, he is drawing power from the infinite "voltage" of the Universal MIND.

But in the human being, the Universal Mind takes on two different aspects. One aspect includes the direction of activities pertaining to man's normal material environment exterior to himself. Therefore we call it the *objective* mind. Sometimes we speak of it as the *"conscious* mind." It is simply that part of our thoughts that we direct upon outward things, necessary to our mortal, mundane or material welfare.

The other portion of the Universal Mind within each of us takes charge of the direction and utilization of forces that operate independently of our conscious or objective phase of mind. Among other things, it directs the functions of respiration, digestion, and all the automatic functions of the body that sustain life and that go on without our cognizance. This phase of the Universal Mind within us we term the *"subjective,"* sometimes called *"subconscious."*

In the human body the objective mind controls the cerebrospinal nervous system. The subjective mind works through the sympathetic nervous system. These two systems are almost entirely separate EXCEPT that the vagus nerve ties the two systems together in one place. The fibres of one system actually join and fuse into the fibres of the other system in the vagus nerve.

Thus the two — subjective and objective — are physically one, but ordinarily are occupied in different ways, the subjective with the various activities of sustaining life and promoting growth, and the objective with receiving the reports of the senses and with reasoning, et cetera.

The junction of the two systems in the vagus

nerve is a two-way valve, so to speak. The stream of force can go EITHER way, or even both ways at the same time. You might conceive of their connection as being like a revolving door at the entrance to a building; through the same door you can go from the building into the street, or vice versa, and different persons can go in opposite directions at the same time through the same door.

This distinction between objective and subjective mind is extremely important. What we have had to say about it so far can be found in any standard book on psychology, but you can easily prove the distinction for yourself without reference to some other person's ideas. Let's do it now.

You know that at this minute you are reading. Certain ideas are being presented to you, and you are considering them. This activity is going on in the *objective* phase of Universal Mind operating through you.

You also know that right at this minute your heart is pumping blood through your veins and arteries. But your thinking mind has nothing to do with that action. That is one example of the activity of the subjective phase of Universal Mind operating through you.

Ordinarily these two phases of mind operate independently (though they are connected). They do not conflict with each other. Yet, from time to time, we find ourselves forced to control the activity of the subjective mind by the action of the objective mind. For instance: We get a stomach ache. That means that the subjective processes of digestion have gone awry. So the objective mind has to step in, select a medicine, and thereby help the subjective mind to do its work properly.

In the foregoing paragraph is contained a very great fact. The objective mind, under certain circumstances, CAN and DOES control the subjective. Likewise the subjective can influence the objective, for the connection works both ways.

There is one more important point for you to note now. When the normal digestive process stops, it is simply because for the time being it has been overtaxed. The subjective mind governing digestion has not *decided* to stop work. It still labors hard to carry digestion on, but a bad food combination overcomes its power. The subjective *cannot* stop its work as long as there is life in the organism. It is *absolutely automatic,* and completely without a will of its own. It can only carry out orders, being unable to distinguish between the correctness or stupidity of those orders.

Your subjective mind has few orders to carry out except those, so to speak, which it received at your birth; these were to carry on the vital functions of breathing, assimilation, digestion, etc., implicit in the very fact of life. But we shall soon see that there are other kinds of orders which *you* can give to the subjective mind, and which it *can* and WILL carry out automatically exactly as ordered.

In the foregoing paragraphs no attempt is made to give explanations conforming to any particular theological doctrines or scientific theories. Nothing has been said that cannot be *proved by you for yourself*. Each statement contains a simple *truth*, stated in such terms that anyone may check it up from his own experience.

Enough has been said already to show that things do not happen to us by chance. There is no such thing as "luck." *Everything* is the *result* of some *cause*, whether that cause be near at hand and easily recognized, such as a crying baby with a pin sticking into it, or remote and seemingly impossible to discover, such as the "injustice" of John Brown's having a better job than you have.

You get pleasant or unpleasant results from your actions depending very largely on how fully you realize and ACT WITH the infinite power of the Universal Mind, of which you are a vehicle for expression. Whether you make that vehicle a powerful twin-six automobile or a one-horse shay depends, from now on, on nobody but *yourself*.

Remember that the one man who has had more influence on the world than anyone else said: "I do nothing of myself." He spoke the truth, probably the greatest single aspect of truth that you and I can realize. Only through the power of Universal Mind could he accomplish the works accredited to him. He, Jesus of Nazareth, knew well how to use that power. And he said that others would do equal or greater things in due time.

Our references to the Nazarene Master, and to other great leaders of the world's thought, have no theological significance. No question of their divinity is involved. We are concerned with them and their utterances solely because they were successful MEN. Their lives and their words may help us in our quest for happiness.

ALL IS ONE

CHAPTER 3

Now we begin to catch a glimmer of what it is that enables some people to succeed far beyond their *apparent* abilities. Remember that we do *not* see their *real* abilities. Perhaps some of those whom we may have envied or called lucky have got hold of this great truth that is beginning to unfold to us in our study of the INVISIBLE CAUSES OF VISIBLE EFFECTS.

We see that all of these invisible causes focus down to the action of the Universal Mind, of which our individual minds are an expression. We see too that these individual minds of ours operate in two ways, subjectively and objectively. And that this subjective mind in each of us *can be controlled* by our objective mind, and that the activity of the subjective mind is directed solely toward carrying out orders, *absolutely automatically*, without any will of its own.

If this ability of the objective to direct the subjective extended only to the usual subjective work of respiration, digestion, etc., such control would scarcely ever be needed, would it? Therefore are we not justified in searching for some other vastly more important reason for its potential control by the objective? Nature does not develop faculties uselessly.

This point will be found to rest on the absolute unity of all things in the Universal Mind, regardless of their apparent physical separateness. This idea is so essential to further understanding of our theme that we shall devote some time now to getting clearly fixed in our consciousness how this can be, and is.

I do not propose to lead you through a maze of metaphysics on this search. So we shall take an illustration or two that will fully explain this idea of unity, and the absolute necessity of realizing it.

You are familiar with a cog wheel. Have you ever realized what a wonderful symbol of cosmic truth it is? Probably not, for we do not ordinarily look for symbols in such commonplace articles. The cog wheel has its hub, spokes, rim and teeth. Now, let the hub represent the Universal Mind. Let each spoke represent a human being, a race, a nation. Call the rim the cycle of life. Let the teeth on the rim represent the individual incidents and experiences of life.

First to engage our attention is the fact that all the spokes have their common origin in the hub— the Universal Mind. The next thing is that *in* that common center of origin each of the spokes contacts and *is a part* of the central hub. Likewise, in the Universal Mind all men, races and nations are ONE and a PART OF EACH OTHER.

But as each spoke goes out toward the rim (toward the cycle of life) it becomes *seemingly* separated and the place where each touches the rim is far apart from its neighbor. I say "seemingly separated," for in REALITY each spoke joins each other spoke in the hub, and each is part of the whole wheel.

Human spokes in the wheel of life too often entertain the false idea that they are separate, that individuality means to be different from each other; right here is where human error begins. The coherent, united nation is all-powerful. Groups of men who work in unity become all-powerful. The individual man who thinks himself a law unto himself *fails.* He has lost his strength in losing his realization of the essential value of unity. Let him recall with Emerson that "everything in Nature contains all the powers of Nature. Everything is made of one hidden stuff."

Now, as a cog wheel revolves, each spoke in turn has to bear its own share of weight and strain. And as each tooth is engaged, representing an incident of experience in the cycle of life, so each human spoke has to bear the full force of that experience, and each human spoke *also receives the transmitted force of the experiences that every other human spoke bears.*

26

Perhaps one human spoke, thinking itself alone, separated from its brethren, deserted, neglected, picked on, feels that it is bearing an undue share of the burden. Really it is not, for it is simply performing its own share, in its own time, obeying the law, "Bear ye one another's burdens." So much for that illustration. Think it over before going on, and realize the ACTUAL *unity* of all *seemingly* separated things.

Now take a sheet of paper. Punch five holes in it and insert your five fingers through them. To a person opposite you, the five fingers represent five separate things. Each finger seems to have the power of individual motion and *seems* to be completely separate and apart from its neighbor. But to *you,* back of the paper, behind the scenes, *beyond the veil* as it were, appears the inescapable FACT that all the fingers *are united;* that they spring from one common unity; that they derive their power from the same source.

Now do you get the point involved? When we get discouraged, when the world seems haywire, when we feel that our backs are to the wall with no help visible, it lowers our ability, our power, our stamina, force and energy, because *we are thinking wrong.* We think we have been cut off from our source. We think ourselves deserted, left alone, badly used, unappreciated, undervalued, unrecognized. We have forgotten the extremely significant FACT that we are ONE with our Creator, ONE in the Universal Mind, ONE with all the creative power in Nature; that we cannot be alone, that we have all the creative and sustaining power in heaven and in earth within us, waiting to be used—*when we know* HOW.

So our very first task in remodeling the things in our lives that do not suit us, is to get fixed fast in our memories this FACT of our Unity with all things in the Universal Mind, for that fact gives us access to far greater powers than any we could ever before imagine as accessible *to* ourselves *by* ourselves.

Do not go on until you realize and ACCEPT that fact. We are coming to the specific details of how to *use* that fact for yourself. But they will do you no good whatsoever unless you *see* the truth of what has been stated up to now.

Go into a huge power station. Observe a great dynamo, capable of generating tremendous power. Its armature may be revolving at an amazing speed. The dynamo is ready for business at a second's notice—the mere pressing of a button or the throwing of a switch. But that huge dynamo is useless until *a demand is made upon it for power*. The moment demand is made by throwing the right switch, the current goes forth over the wires. But the demand MUST BE MADE. Not a unit of power goes forth until that demand makes it possible.

But if you do not know that the dynamo exists, or do not believe it after having been told so, there is no use in telling you *how* to use it, is there?

Now let us bring this picture right home to ourselves. We have the source of power *within ourselves*, ready for business. But no power will come from it to help us do the things we wish to do until we recognize its existence, and make a call on its power and direct it to the desired purpose. There is a specific way in which we can make that demand, a way in which we can set that power to work for us. It is the greatest power in the world, far greater than any dynamo invented by man, for it is the POWER that enabled man to invent the dynamo.

CHAPTER 4

THE GREAT LINK

IF you have followed the discussion carefully so far, you have thoroughly in mind these ideas:

(a) All is One in the Universal Mind.

(b) You personally are an individualized channel for expression of that one Mind.

(c) In your human existence you use that Mind both objectively and subjectively.

(d) Your subjective mind can be controlled by your objective mind, and it carries out orders automatically.

(e) Ordinarily these orders relate to the usual body-regulating functions of the subjective, but it will also act on orders about other types of activity.

Let us now set ourselves definitely to see that there are, in fact, other kinds of orders which the subjective will accept from the objective and CARRY OUT.

To do so we shall adjourn to the vaudeville theater.

There we see a hypnotist at work. By means of a few passes in front of a person's face he gets him under his control. Just what do we mean by "under his control?" This is what we mean: He *disconnects* the hypnotized person's subjective mind from his objective mind, and then the hypnotist *substitutes* his own objective mind to *control* the hypnotized person's subjective mind.

There is no other possible explanation, and the actual fact of hypnosis has been amply demonstrated scientifically.

All right, the hypnotist has *you* under control, let us say. Your objective thinking mind is asleep. You remember absolutely nothing of what is done to you under hypnosis, after you come out of it. Meanwhile the hypnotist has had you under his control, or, to put it more exactly, your bodily functions (ruled by the subjective) have been completely under the control of HIS objective mind. This is extremely important. Simply by ordering you to run around the stage and bark like a dog, he has *made* you do so. Your subjective mind does not ask itself *why* it should cause your body to act like a dog—it *automatically* accepts the order given it and immediately carries it out to the best of its ability, either at once or as soon as it is able to do so.

There is scarcely any limit to what the subjective mind can be made to do, in this manner.

Now you perhaps see more clearly why we have said that the subjective mind receives orders and acts on them *automatically*, without arguing as to their sense. Certainly if some other person, such as a hypnotist, can impress his will on your subjective mind, you yourself can do the same thing *much more easily with your own objective mind.*

One other important point is found in our study of the hypnotist. Ordinarily *your* subjective mind is only dealing with *your own* objective mind. But it *can* deal with somebody else's objective mind *without knowing the difference.* Otherwise the hypnotist could not control you. Your subjective mind is therefore entirely impersonal. That is only another way of saying that your subjective mind is *universal* in its reactions—it does *not* discriminate as to persons, or reasons why, or pros and cons.

How different in this respect is your objective mind! It is very keenly aware of the difference between persons. It sifts reasons. It argues pros and cons. It definitely *does* discriminate. Hence your objective mind is *not* universal in its use by you—it is decidedly *specific,* and rightly so for being of use on the plane of the specific, or, in other words, the world in which you live.

Now we are ready to take the big step forward.

We have already found that the basic source of all power on all planes—physical, mental or emotional—is in the Universal Mind.

Now we have just discovered that only one aspect of your mind's activity—the subjective—is *likewise universal* in its reactions.

Hence we see that your individualized SUBJEC-

TIVE MIND IS YOUR IMMEDIATE PERSONAL LINK WITH THE UNIVERSAL MIND. It is your GREAT LINK with all else that is.

And since all things are possible to the Universal Mind, the power of an individual expression of that Universal Mind—such as *your own subjective mind* —is limited only by the arbitrary conditions of time, space, force and the other natural laws under which you as a human being are limited. *But it has no further limitations.*

In other words, your subjective mind could not cause you to rise up from the chair where you are sitting and float about the room. It could not cause you to expand instantaneously to a height of twenty feet. It could not enable you to scratch your right elbow with your right hand. All those things are physically impossible, made so in our arbitrary world of time and space.

But your subjective mind, having access to the vast power of the *Universal* Subjective Mind, can accomplish ANYTHING which is not prohibited by the laws of time and space. To be specific—it can make your body strong and well. It can attract to you the kind of life mate that you want. It can make you a capable citizen of your community, with proper compensation to you for your services. It can, in short, make you successful and happy.

How it does so comes next.

But don't go on to that until you are sure you understand the trend of our thought so far. Do you see—truly—that you are an expression of Universal Mind? Do you realize that this is made manifest in you through your subjective mind? Do you see why this subjective mind can accomplish anything for you that is not contrary to the laws of our world? And, finally, do you recall that your subjective mind is under the control of your objective mind, ready to obey it down to the last detail?

If you have come so far without lagging behind you are now ready to take the most important step of all. In fact, you have probably anticipated me and done it already.

Chapter 5

FORMING THE PICTURE

Again let us review briefly what we have done so far. We have found that:

(a) As Shelley says, "Nothing in this world is single, all things by a law divine, in each other's being mingle." In other words, All is One in what we term Universal Mind. Seeming separateness is an illusion of the senses.

(b) Each of us is an individual expression of that Universal Mind. It functions in us both outwardly, through our objective mind, and inwardly, through our subjective mind. These are really but two aspects of the One Mind, but they function differently because of our nature.

(c) Your objective mind, circumscribed in its abilities by your experience, your judgment and your mentality in its outward dealings with THIS world, has but limited power. But your subjective mind, directed inwardly to ALL THE WORLDS on inner planes, drawing life from the very source of *everything that is,* has access to UNLIMITED POWER.

(d) Despite the incredible difference in their respective potential powers, your objective mind can control your subjective mind, give it orders and plan its activities. So it sets at work for you (by consciously cooperating with your subjective mind) infinitely greater forces than your comparatively feeble conscious mentality can command alone.

All this we have now checked up on, and you must be satisfied so far, or the rest of our discussion will prove a total loss to you.

Our next step: to discover *how* the objective can control the subjective . . . how, in other words, can we *consciously create circumstances?*

Through our five senses we distinguish objects in our visible world according to what we call "form." If we look at a picture or a landscape, we see the form it presents by means of our eyes and brain. If we close our eyes, we can still preserve that picture by a *"mental vision" of what we have seen.* But the picture we see with our eyes and later reproduce in our minds is the picture of something that *already* exists. It is the result of some *previous* creative activity.

Now approaches the big point to which we have been working since we first began this study. *In consciously creating circumstances we reverse the process of physical sight.* Instead of seeing mentally a picture of what we know already exists physically, we use this giant power within us by impressing our individual subjective mind WITH THE PICTURE OF WHAT WE WANT TO SEE COME ABOUT PHYSICALLY.

That is how simple it is. Simple, I said, not easy . . . but entirely POSSIBLE.

When we view a picture or landscape, we see it

first with our physical eyes, then in our minds. Now throw the gears into reverse. In your work of consciously creating circumstances you are to see the picture of what you want *first in your* MIND, and later with your physical eye after it comes into externalization.

You originate pictures and then, by means of a definite technique, you make them come true before your very eyes, in due time.

Put another way, creating circumstances requires you first to impress on your subjective mind what you want to perceive later with your objective mind.

This is a revolutionary thought to some people. "How can you reverse a natural process," they say, "and expect to get results?" Well, you do it with other natural processes. You can make your automobile go backward—even though it usually goes forward. You can make the electric motor run the steam engine, although it usually works vice versa. And the sun itself first turns day into night, and then turns night into day.

So too, you, a son or daughter of the sun, can turn your dark night of trouble, of discord, disappointments and delays into the glorious day of accomplishment, joy and happiness by *reversing the usual process*. Do not wait to accept whatever may come before your eyes! Determine for yourself what SHALL come before your eyes! You CAN and WILL DO IT, if you will follow directions.

But, first and foremost, KNOW WHAT YOU WANT. Many people fail in life because they do not realize what they want. Have a clear, well-defined understanding with yourself before you start consciously to create circumstances.

Do not make up your mind hastily. In dealing with an infinite force you cannot afford to be hasty; if you insist on being so, you will have only yourself to blame when your efforts fail, as they surely will. YOU CANNOT HURRY THE INFINITE!

Now let us say that you have a particular desire. We will assume that it is a desire that you can, with the warm approval of your conscience, take to the Universal Mind for fulfillment. How do you get results?

To some extent we all enjoy a faculty of "imagination," which Einstein has said is more important than knowledge. Imagination differs in degree and in kind in the individual according to temperament, vocation and evolutional status, but wherever there is human consciousness there also is *some* degree of imagination. So, when you have a distinct desire you automatically form a mental picture of it; incomplete as it may be, it requires the use of your imaging faculty.

Having satisfied yourself that your predominating desire is worthy, that it involves no harm or detriment to another, and that it will work out to the advantage of others besides yourself FIX THAT DESIRE. Use your imagination to the utmost to develop a perfect, well-defined picture of it, not as you hope it may be, but AS IF IT WERE ALREADY A FACT. See yourself in that picture actually occupied in doing exactly what you would do if it were already externalized. Hold this mental picture as long as you can. Concentrate on making the image complete. *Do not strain or try to will it into being.* Just keep the image in mind, thinking of it objectively as often as your activities permit.

Now what are you really doing? Clearly, you are using your *objective* mind to decide what you want and to build up a perfect picture of that desire brought about in your life. Lots of people go that far.

But here is where 999 out of 1000 go wrong. They make the objective mind, greatly limited in its knowledge and power, try to do the rest of the job which properly belongs to the subjective mind, with its direct access to the *unlimited* power and knowledge of the Universal Mind.

Once you have formed your picture objectively, give the poor tired conscious mentality a rest. Leave the remainder of the job to the Universal. Not as a request or a hope that it will see you through, but in perfect faith, born of *knowledge,* that your image has already been built and is bound to come to pass.

Why should you have that faith? Why will your images, if persisted in and adhered to constantly, come true in the circumstances of your daily life? What, so to speak, are the mechanics of the process?

Let's go back a little.

We agreed that the objective can control the subjective, which means that an image formed by the objective can be impressed on the subjective *as an order to be carried out.* The hypnotist orders the unconscious person under his conscious control to bark like a dog; his subject barks like a dog. Your unconscious (subjective) mind receives an order from your conscious (objective) mind, for instance, to make you well, get you money, or whatnot: your subjective mind immediately accepts the order and goes to work.

What tools does the subjective mind have to work with? My answer is: *all* the tools, known and unknown, in the universe, because it is *your personal link* with the Universal Subjective Mind which knows all, sees all, and can accomplish all things. And it WILL do whatever you command, because it is impersonal and has no will of its own, any more than a great reservoir can refuse to let the water run out of a single spigot that is turned on.

40

Therefore you can entirely, with reason, have the faith that your demand will be met, that your images will come to pass in your own life, that the circumstances you consciously create mentally will come about physically just as surely as you are reading these words. For, as Disraeli asserted, "Man is not the creature of circumstances. Circumstances are the creatures of men."

These images we generally term "thought-forms" because they ARE real forms in the world of thought. You decide *objectively* what they shall be. You work *subjectively* to bring them about. Do not confuse the two. Let each aspect of mind do the work it can do best.

The ways and means of doing so come next.

CHAPTER 6

IMPRESSING YOUR DESIRE

WE WILL assume that a desire has taken shape in your mind, due to the absence of something in your life or environment that must be supplied to complete your happiness or welfare. That desire has been picturized by your imagination as a definite thought-form. All this has taken place in your objective mind.

Your next step is to impress this thought-form upon your subjective mind, for there *the real work begins*. Talk to your subjective mind as though it were directly to an individual. Some people find it helpful to direct their speech toward the solar plexus, for the reason that the solar plexus, or center of your subjective mind, is the individual's link with Universal Mind. To us the most important thing in the outside Universe is the sun, giver of life, center of our system. That is why the solar plexus is very aptly named. Some call the solar plexus the "abdominal brain," for it represents the seat of activities that go on independently of the conscious brain.

When you speak to your subjective mind you may do so mentally, if you prefer, or if audible speech would be disconcerting to others. But if possible, do so audibly to assist in crystallizing your thought-form.

When you speak to your subjective mind, close your eyes—not for any weird or occult reason, but simply that your mind may not be diverted by the sight of things in your environment that provoke distraction of thought.

In the darkness of closed eyes, try to FEEL that which you cannot see, namely the subtle body of the Universal Mind flowing through your organism. Realize the truth of the Scriptural statement that "In Him we live and move and have our being," for it is a basic scientific FACT. If it were not so, we could have no existence at all. If you do not bring yourself at first to this definite *feeling*, at least bring yourself to the state of mind in which you accept it as unseen, unfelt, but incontrovertibly TRUE.

Then, with your eyes closed, bring the picture of your thought-form to mind, and describing it clearly, speak to your subjective mind, which you conceive of as in the solar plexus. Say something like this to your subjective mind: "It is my *desire* and my *will* that you do thus and so, using me as a focal center of attraction. It is a worthy request. I ask it unselfishly. I desire to be in perfect harmony with all constructive activity. I KNOW you have the power to bring about what I order through your connection with the all-powerful Universal Mind. YOU ARE DOING IT NOW, and I thank you for hearing me." Never forget to give thanks, even as the Great Master said, "I thank thee, Father, that thou hast heard me." What is worth having is worthy of thanks.

Your subjective mind, being a function of the Universal Subjective Mind, then impresses the image with which you have charged it upon the potency of the whole body of the Universal Mind with you as a focal center. By the Law of Attraction the elements necessary to the externalization of your thought-form in your life are built up. To put it simply, the thought-form comes true, because this archetypal mental form must build a corresponding set of circumstances in the world of matter.

We say that your subjective mind impresses the image with which it is charged upon the whole body of the Universal Mind. Let us clarify the statement a bit. If you have a basin or container of strong acid, such as sulphuric, you know that any part of that acid is as potent as any other. If you dip in a splinter of wood at any place, it will be burned by the strong acid. The splinter does not contact *all* the acid at once, but all the power of the acid in the container exists at any point of contact. If you dip another splinter into the acid at the same time at another point the same result takes place.

So it is with the Universal Mind. All the POWER of that Universal Mind is brought to focus at any point at which it may be contacted, and the results at one point will be equally present at any other point. The acid is just as strong at whatsoever points it may be contacted, even if many points contact it at the same time. This is equally true of the Universal Mind.

When talking to your subjective mind, remember one thing above all. *Do not attempt to tell it its own business, which is the means of carrying out your order.* It knows far more than you can possibly know. It manipulates forces that you cannot even dream of. Let it do its work in its own way. Make your order as simple, clear and uninvolved as possible. The clearer and simpler your charge, the quicker will you attain results. Just give the plain outlines of what you want to realize. *Do not limit the subjective as to time.* Do not stipulate how or through what channels your money, your friendship, your job or what not is to come. Hold fast only to the image itself, and the details will be filled in later.

The principal matter to keep in mind at this stage is the necessity of sublime faith. We are not teaching "faith-cures" or anything of the sort. What you are learning is based absolutely upon *knowledge and fact.* But faith plays an important part in all human experience. If you asked a friend to do something for you and then began to question whether he would be *able* to do so, if you began to *hope* that he might, or *fear* that in some way he would not, how much do you think that friend would do for you if he knew just how you felt? Well, the Universal knows far more about how you feel than any human being could possibly know, because you are a part of the Universal, and you therefore communicate every state of mind within you to the Universal Mind, even though you do so unconsciously. Therefore you must not doubt its ability, no matter how great a demand you make on it.

Do you wonder whether you can really impress a picture of your desire or "thought-form" upon the Universal Mind? Why not? Any teacher of psychology in a recognized institution will inform you very quickly that the ability to impress thoughts in one mind upon another mind has been demonstrated *over and over again.* In our present discussion we are not dealing with the cumbersome faculties of human individuals but with the all-potent medium of the Universal Mind itself, upon which all the thoughts of all the individuals through all the ages have been impressed.

The technique we have given is simple. The results will depend entirely upon the mental attitude and spiritual trust you can develop. *Do not worry about results.* Let them take care of themselves. They will manifest according to your ability to

46

contact the Universal Mind in an attitude of understanding and true faith. If you must have faith in your fellow man in order to draw from him the best that is in him, how much more should you have faith in the Unseen Power that is Father to us all!

Let us see if we can make all this more practical by an example. This to my personal knowledge was actually accomplished by what we have been talking about—consciously creating circumstances.

A man wanted to sell a house. This was in the midst of our late lamented depression—perhaps not so late. Naturally his chances of selling the house seemed slim, by ordinary standards. Houses were not being bought. This man knew he was up against it. Yet he *had* to sell the house. What did he do?

First of all, he did what he could with his objective mind. He placed the house in the hands of three brokers. So much anyone would have done.

But this person did a great deal more. He built up a complete picture of the house already sold. Notice, not the details of selling it or the kind of people who would buy it. But a picture of the thing accomplished—of himself packing up, seeing the moving vans come in, load up and drive away, and then driving away in his own car and waving goodbye to the house for the last time. He thought of all this as *already* a fact on the mental plane. He concentrated on that image, almost eating and sleeping with it. Beyond his original listing with the brokers, he did little with his objective mind about selling the house. But all the while his subjective— or rather the *Universal* Subjective Mind—was busy about its job, accepting his command and carrying it out.

In that month there were dozens of houses advertised for sale in his community. Only two were sold. One was my friend's. And his thought-form came true down to the last detail, even to his waving good-bye to the house when he drove away.

I think the point is clear. Many more examples could be given and will be suggested in our further discussions.

The great majority of people, through ignorance or lack of faith, use a child's tin hammer to drive home their desires when they could use a ten-ton pile driver. They put a toy electric motor behind their ambitions when they could harness up a giant turbine. In other words, they use only their confused, helter-skelter, feeble *objective* minds when they could tap the infinite resources of the *Universal Subjective Mind*.

Why should you remain among the unenlightened? The law is simple, positive, definite: "Ask and it shall be given unto you; seek and ye shall find; knock and it shall be opened unto you." That means you. Thousands have demonstrated its truth.

You can, too. You now know the meaning of that grand promise.

CHAPTER 7

THE LAW OF ATTRACTION

HERE let us pause to survey more closely the *means* by which your thought-form, correctly evolved and stamped on the Universal Mind, will become manifest in the facts of your life.

We have already discussed the point, but it will be well here to study further, and *understand,* the great Law of Attraction on which depends the success of your thought-forms.

It is a law in physics that "unlikes attract, and likes repel," meaning of course "polarities," the term used to express opposites.

We are used to this expression in dealing with electricity and magnetism, but by careful observation we shall find that this law operates throughout Nature's entire domain. Now note carefully how we make the law operative in accordance with our *legitimate* and *reasonable* desires as expressed in thought-forms.

Universal Substance manifests the two polarities of Matter and Spirit, and as a corollary to that fact, formations in the invisible mental and spiritual worlds seek manifestation in the visible material world. In this search for material expression Nature's forces generate and develop tremendous activity and this activity is the cause of all action and reaction, urging and restraining, positive and negative, in cosmos. It produces the phenomenon we ordinarily call "life."

The principle holds true in regard to your thought-form. First you formulate and develop it on the inner, invisible plane. Then the invisible thought-form, which is the positive polarity, seeks the negative polarity or material expression of itself. All that is visible in the mundane world about us, is the expression of the activity of invisible archetypes in the inner worlds.

If you have ever watched frost crystals form on a window pane during cold weather, you will have noticed how the lines of crystallization radiate in very definite directions, always in geometrically correct proportions of balance and symmetry— a fine illustration of Nature's maintenance of equilibrium.

Your thought-form operates in exactly the same manner. In the case of the frost crystal, we *see* the lines of crystallization becoming visible and these lines are called the "lines of force," i.e., the direction taken by the operative force in crystallizing the moisture. Your thought-form does the same thing. You cannot see it visibly in just the same way as you see the frost crystals, but you *can* see it by observing carefully the various incidents in your daily life, which will become apparent to you as indicating just how conditions are shaping themselves toward the ultimate realization of your desire.

Little by little, you will note apparently insuperable obstacles being eliminated, providing you with *greater scope and opportunity,* with the way being made clearer for you to *progress* toward your goal.

The frost crystal does not spring into visible manifestation instantaneously; neither will the realization of your thought-form. The frost crystal is a manifestation wherein the constructive material is of the most attenuated character. Your thought-form is complex, involving a vast array of constructive materials, and possibly also involving other individuals, and much time is necessarily required for the operative activities to bring all the elements together in visible realization.

But the realization will surely come, if you are patient and persistent and, above all, conscientious. Lines of force will radiate out from your growing thought-form just as the tiny roots radiate out from the fast-growing plant or shrub. These roots radiate in ever-widening areas in search of nourishment, and that nourishment consists of material substances which they can assimilate.

The length of time necessary for the thought-form to "come true" will depend on its nature; whether it is simple or complex, whether it involves just you or others, whether the obstacles to be overcome are few or many.

The two factors of thought-forms and the Law of Attraction are the prime working tools of the mental scientist, and on them depend the amazing phenomena of metaphysics, psychology and mental science.

There is an interesting and true analogy between the workings of a thought-form and the growth of a plant which will help you to understand this extremely important point of *why* thought-forms "come true."

A tiny seed is planted in the ground. You plant it, let us say. Probably, if you are wise in such matters, you first clear away stones, weeds and rubbish from your garden. You select the seed carefully, studying the different grades or brands offered to get just the flower you want.

After planting the seed, you see that it has the right conditions for growth, including moisture and *freedom from disturbance*. In the dark earth the creative processes of nature—which you cannot see — are bringing the seed along, and soon comes the day when it pokes its bright green shoot above ground.

Sunlight, moisture, air and, again, *freedom from disturbance*, eventually bring the plant to full growth, and the beautiful flower spreads its fragrance for you *and others* to enjoy.

Obviously the seed is the thought-form. You select it carefully—either the seed or thought-form —to make sure it is the *one* you want. You prepare the ground for your thought-form by clearing away the stones of envy, the weeds of sloth and discontent, and the rubbish of belief in limitation.

You stamp the thought-form in the Universal (plant the seed in the earth) carefully and earnestly. Then, just as you do not disturb the seed after planting, you do not disturb the thought-form by doubting its power, or by fussing with its details.

And just as the invisible powers of nature cause the seed to sprout, so do the equally invisible powers of the Universal cause your thought-form to "sprout." You cooperate with Nature by providing moisture and possibly fertilizer for the invisible seed; likewise you cooperate with the Universal by providing *meditation* and a calm, sure *expectancy* that the thought-form *will* sprout.

And inevitably one day the first tiny shoot of the thought-form will become visible, that is, the first specific result of it will appear in your life. Glad day! From then on, if you continue to aid it with the life-giving waters of *meditation* and hearten it with *sunny* expectation of its eventual completion, it will continue to grow, and sooner or later it will stand forth in your life an accomplished fact. And, like the flower, it will gladden OTHERS as well as yourself.

Really, are thought-forms and their working out any more miraculous than the sprouting of a seed? They are both based on the Law of Attraction. We are used to the one, unused to the other, that is all. But think how great was the amazement of the first man who planted a seed of wheat, and later found it growing into a plant that would nourish him! In those days it required *real* FAITH to take the trouble to plant, when no results were immediately apparent. And today it requires the same faith to plant a thought-form, at least until you KNOW FROM EXPERIENCE that they *do* sprout.

But this faith is just the one thing you MUST have, and we have seen the logical basis for it in this explanation of the Law of Attraction. This fundamental requirement of the individual's *belief* is well summed up in the Master's words: "Therefore, I say unto you, What things soever ye desire, when ye pray, believe that ye receive them, and ye shall receive them." Now surely it is difficult to believe that we have received something, when our senses tell us to the contrary. Yet this is *absolutely neces-sary* for the individual who seeks success through the use of thought-forms.

It certainly seems like "putting the cart before

the horse." Nevertheless it is quite sound, and to the extent that we can bring our consciousness to an undertanding and acceptance of this truth will our results be successful or unsuccessful.

We may resort to another illustration to clarify the point. When we take a photograph of a landscape, the momentary flash of light has imprinted the picture of the subject on the sensitive plate *permanently*. As long as that plate lasts, many positives or prints may be made from it. That is what the plate or film was made for. The landscape may change with the seasons or by the hand of man, but the print of it on the negative will be preserved as long as the owner of the camera desires to keep it. Likewise, when you impress or "imprint" your thought-form on the sensitive Universal Mind, you have *at once* imprinted it on a medium that is *eternal*. It can never be destroyed.

And since the Universal Mind is eternal, and your thought-form therefore imperishable, *it has begun to work instantly*. With the Infinite and Eternal, to know and to act are one and the same. Therefore, what you have asked for HAS come into being at once, and you may logically believe that you *have* received it, although the realization of your reception of it will be delayed until it has been brought into physical manifestation, when the time is ripe. This is shown us in Scripture, where the Master prayed and then *immediately* thanked the Father saying: "I know that thou hast heard me." He thanked the Father *before* he visibly received the things for which He had asked.

So we may interpolate our own words in the Master's injunction to make its meaning immediately obvious: "What things soever ye desire, when ye pray (impress your thought-form), believe that ye receive them (in the invisible world, immediately), and *ye shall* receive them" (in the visible world, later on, through the Law of Attraction between invisible and visible).

CHAPTER 8

BREAD UPON THE WATERS

WHEN YOU *personally* begin to study the use of thought-forms and begin to make them part of your mental equipment, shaping circumstances by them consciously, you will have taken a tremendous step forward—perhaps the most significant single step forward that you ever will take.

You will then have begun to take the first steps in the kindergarten of conscious creation. You will naturally stumble and fall, probably cry a bit, but then you will try again and sooner or later accomplish the first steps. I promise you, my friend, that few things on earth equal the joy you will get from learning that first lesson. When you know that this marvelous new power is YOURS—you will sing for joy. You will then *know* that all things in Heaven and Earth are yours to command. That you yourself can solve your own problems, be they what they may. That you have within yourself the seeds of your own success.

This may sound exaggerated if you have not learned that first lesson. Yet I *know, personally,* scores of men and women *of only average mental equipment* who have learned this lesson. Once gained it can never be lost, no matter how slowly or with what difficulty the further lessons are mastered.

And the very fact that you are reading these words and thinking about these mysteries, for they *are* mysteries, demonstrates that you personally are marching in the vanguard of evolution, because very few people know about the power of thought-forms.

Nature wastes nothing. If you had not earned the right to know about thought-forms, you would not hear of them! If your past had not brought you to the point where you could accept this great power and use it, you would not be told about it. The very fact that you know about this throbbing dynamo waiting for you to throw the switch is proof that you are entitled to use its power.

Whether you use it is, of course, entirely up to you. "Many are called, but few are chosen." That might better read, "Many are called, but few choose." I do not ask you whether you want this power, or urge you to take it. In fact, I warn you that use of this power for evil ends will hurt you badly.

Do not hesitate to use thought-forms because of a fear that your *method* will be wrong. That will not hurt you. You simply will not get results, in that case, and no harm is done. But BE SURE that your thought-forms do not intend any harm to another person, because that will inevitably react on you quite unpleasantly, as we shall discover later on.

Here is the inner significance of "casting your bread upon the waters." After many days it *shall* come back unto you. The bread is your thought-form. The waters are the infinite ocean of subjective mind, containing all power to transform that thought-form into actual earthly conditions.

That is how you consciously create circumstances.

And if you would ask just how to begin to use this vast power—what kind of a thought-form to fashion first—I would suggest this:

Immediately set to work to clean out of your heart any bitter, destructive, unkind, uncharitable feelings. You cannot build a new house with rubbish from the old one cluttering up the lot.

When you are satisfied that you have honestly done that, begin to build up an image of yourself as a conscious agent of Universal Mind, receiving inspiration from the source of all things to aid you and others in making life more worth living. Some find it helpful in forming a picture of this kind to imagine themselves receiving floods of light and power from the Sun, and this is a good method, for the Sun blesses us with much besides daylight and warmth.

But I shall not go into particulars about the details of this basic thought-form of yours. If I did, it would be mine, not yours. Meditate on the idea. Let it mature in your own mind. When you are satisfied with it, adopt it definitely and see it already DONE. Add to it from time to time if additional details occur to you. Concentrate on it whenever you can.

The important point is your realization of yourself as an instrument of Universal Mind. A feeble instrument now, perhaps, but one that can build itself into a bigger, finer person by surveying your possibilities, and then consciously developing them as you will be instructed.

Work first on your basic thought-form. Never mind that specific want in your life that needs to be filled. That will be taken care of more quickly if you first make sure of your *general* alignment with nature's constructive forces.

In passing, let us clear up one point. We began this study by saying that successful people have access to something that failures do not know about. Now we are talking about thought-forms. Does that mean that *all* successful people use thought-forms? By no means; or rather, they do not all use them *consciously*. But even if they are used unconsciously, they have *some* power.

Electrical engineers know that a current of electricity flowing through one wire will *induce* a current in a wire laid alongside it, even though the second wire is not connected with it or to any battery. The effect is *slight,* and as nothing compared with the current in the first wire, but it exists.

In a similar way, a strong image of a desire in one's objective mind will have *some* effect on one's subjective mind, even though it is not *consciously* impressed on it as a thought-form. The results will be minor compared with the results of *consciously* stamping the thought-form. It is this unconscious activity, small though it is, that has enabled many people to achieve success, because they knew what they wanted, and they wanted it vigorously.

Theodore Roosevelt had a bold vision of a canal across the Isthmus of Panama. French engineers had failed to build it after the expenditure of millions. Roosevelt knew the idea was good. It was unselfish. It meant far-reaching good for his country. So he held the idea firmly in mind, against considerable opposition. The canal was dug, and America has blessed him ever since.

Napoleon once exclaimed, when asked about certain circumstances: "Circumstances?—I MAKE circumstances." So can you—but you can avoid his tragic personal destiny by being constructive.

The deaf Beethoven never heard his later marvelous symphonies, but who doubts that his more sensitized inner ear was attuned to symphonies that few of us could ever hope to hear? He so strongly desired to bring at least a part of them over to us that we of later years revere his memory.

The elder Roebling got an idea for building bridges from watching spiders. No one had ever had it before. But the idea became so strong with him that it finally took objective shape in the Brooklyn Bridge.

I doubt whether any of these successful men had any conception of a thought-form *as such*, yet they accomplished great things through the mere inductive effect of their strong desires, plus, of course, native ability. They used thought-forms unconsciously. Anyone with *average* ability who uses THOUGHT-FORMS *consciously* can work wonders as remarkable in his life as did these great ones with their superior natural ability who used thought-forms unconsciously.

"No pleasure is comparable to the standing upon the vantage-ground of truth," asserted Francis Bacon, and the beginner in using thought-forms has not long to wait before he appreciates the significance of this claim by one of the greatest minds of all ages.

Chapter 9

ENTERING THE KINGDOM

Now let us review again, briefly, to be sure that we understand each other so far.

Each of us functions mentally in a dual fashion. Objectively we work through our brain, with its powers of observation, comparison, reasoning and imagination — relating to things on our limited mundane plane. Subjectively, we work through our solar plexus, with its access to the unlimited power of the Universal Subjective Mind.

Your brain can direct the activities of your solar plexus—or, to put it another way, your objective can direct your subjective mind. For convenience we speak of these as two minds, though in reality they are but different expressions of the one mind.

By deciding objectively what *shall* come into your life, and impressing the picture of that desire forcefully on your subjective, you can bring about those conditions as you wish, before your very eyes, in due time.

These images which we impress on the subjective we call thought-forms. The process of using them we call "consciously creating circumstances." The successful people of this world are chiefly distinguished from the laggards by reason of their use of thought-forms—consciously or otherwise.

This takes us in outline through our previous discussions. Now let us go on to further details of your basic thought-form. You are probably anxious for me to give you specific suggestions about how to get a job, or a better job; money, a wife or husband. But please listen to me: do *not* form any *specific* thought-form for a while. Stick to the basic, general thought-form. It won't be easy to be patient. But it *will* be worth while.

Let me give you seven reminders:

(1) Make your thought-form constructive.

(2) Include benefit to others as well as yourself.

(3) Make it practical.

(4) Concentrate it on what you want to BE or DO—*not* on what you want to *have*.

(5) Visualize the thought-form as worked out NOW.

(6) Make the thought-form relate to YOURSELF as the agent of Good.

(7) Act constantly in full faith that your thought-form *is* working out.

Your life can be just as wonderful as *you* decide to make it. Now keep that brain of yours quiet, with its habitual objections and doubts and hesitations. I repeat, YOUR LIFE CAN BE JUST AS WONDERFUL AS YOU DECIDE TO MAKE IT — provided only that you use the truths which the real YOU does not need to be convinced of—*for it already knows them—*

but which the shell you call your body needs to be stirred into using ACTIVELY.

All power in Heaven or on Earth is yours individually to command! Yes, I said ALL power.

The great laws of the Universe have brought YOU to the point, after eons of eons, where, as a self-conscious, individualized entity, you have had the *key* to Nature's great storehouse *put right into your palm*. Can't you almost feel it burning your flesh with its *divine fire?* Can't you hear its stirring message that says: "Come, my friend and brother, USE me! There is nothing that shall be held back from you when once I have turned the lock. Let my golden substance turn this world into the Kingdom of Heaven for you NOW."

Here, to some, may be an impious thought. If you consider the Kingdom of Heaven something to be hoped for *after death,* but not to be aspired to during this life—banish that thought instantly and forever. The Kingdom of Heaven is *everywhere,* available at *all* times to those who seek it. And "let not him that seeketh cease from his search until he find," says the Master, "and when he finds he shall wonder, and wondering he shall reach the kingdom, and when he reaches the kingdom, he shall have rest."

I would suggest for your serious consideration that we have been discussing the Kingdom of

Heaven by another name. I wonder whether you have spotted it under the cloak of analysis we have thrown around it.

Yes, my friend, one aspect of the Kingdom of Heaven is the Universal Mind.

Now I want you to stop reading this book in a moment and *do* something.

I want you to build up for yourself a picture of whatever you as a subject of the Kingdom of Heaven on Earth would ask in the way of powers, joys, happiness. Make the picture as nearly perfect as your imagination can conceive. Keep it on this earth, remember, because this is *practical*. And make it helpful for OTHERS as well as yourself.

Go ahead now—do it. Never mind why. We are going to stop while you build up that picture. Put yourself mentally into the Kingdom of Heaven on Earth. Seriously. Do not read further for the next five or ten minutes, while you concentrate on a picture of what the Kingdom of Heaven on Earth would mean to you.

All right. Now you have just created your BASIC PERMANENT THOUGHT-FORM. So far you have only created it consciously — with your objective mind. *Hold fast to it.* Perhaps you will want to write it down.

But that is only part of the process. Now let's complete it. You are now to speak mentally to your subjective mind — concentrating on your solar plexus as your link to Universal Mind. Impress it with that picture of yourself in the Kingdom of Heaven on Earth as powerfully as you know how. Never mind whether you are doing it *just* right. You are making a start. You will do this many, many times more!

Say to your REAL self mentally: "This is what I desire to be. All power is yours to create those circumstances. You *have* created them in the world of thought. I joyfully await their manifestation in the objective world, for lo! my own shall come to me."

Do that right now. Do not go on for even one paragraph until you have done so.

Now I suggest for your most serious consideration that *you have just entered the Kingdom of Heaven*. You have just taken one of the most wonderful steps a human being can master — even *greater* in its satisfaction than the pleasure the proud parents take in Junior's first step on this plane.

And like Junior, you will probably stumble and fall and cry right afterward. But that need not bother you. Junior goes on to stride manfully across the room, and out into the great world to take his rightful place — and so WILL YOU learn to walk boldly in the Kingdom of Heaven on Earth and take your rightful place in it. In it there are many mansions! *One of them is yours*, and it will be built for you by the Great Architect of the Universe *exactly according to your specifications.*

And here we are again back with our old friend the thought-form.

It is the basic thought-form which *you* establish that supplies the specifications of that mansion of yours in the Kingdom of Heaven on Earth. It is the infinite power of the Universal Subjective Mind that builds the mansion for you, and when it is ready, throws it open to your possession. You decide what shall be created for you. Then you *hold fast* to that image: you *keep out* contrary or diluting ideas; you *"stay your haste"* knowing that your own shall come to you; and you *remember* that "no wind can drive your bark astray," as John Burroughs wrote.

And as surely as the sun shall rise tomorrow, you shall live in your mansion of the Kingdom of Heaven on Earth *in this life,* if you hold fast to the basic thought-form that you have just built.

One of Oliver Wendell Holmes' most inspired stanzas develops this thought:

"Build thee more stately mansions, O my soul,

As the swift seasons roll!

Leave thy low-vaulted past!

Let each new temple, nobler than the last,

Shut thee from heaven with a dome more vast,

69

Till thou at length art free,
Leaving thine outgrown shell by life's unresting sea!"

The mental scientist is engaged in this process.

Every human being comes to his individual Garden of Gethsemane; every human individual treads the Via Dolorosa. Every human individual comes, sooner or later, to his Golgotha. Your worries, your distress, sufferings or problems may be the Golgotha that is intended to turn your inner consciousness toward the Light—toward the Sun whose rays shine through the inspired ideas of mental science. The problems which you doubtless have you should be thankful for, for have they not been the agency of exposing you to these TRUTHS?

All power, both in heaven and on earth, is *yours* to use, if you seek it wisely, unselfishly and constructively. Your beginnings may be small, but they will be obvious to you in many ways that will encourage you if you heed the little things. Be not greedy for the big things immediately. The *big things will come in due time* and that time of waiting will be a test of your faith and your "endurance unto the end."

One swallow does not make a summer, nor can one or two minutes spent on a constructive thought-form undo the destructive influence of the countless weakening thoughts you may have *ignorantly* and *unconsciously* sent into Universal Mind for years.

70

Yet a beginning must be made somewhere and at some time. If you have participated actively in our little exercises, you have made an excellent beginning.

Now, how shall you continue and what shall you do to bring this effort to fruition? What must you be sure to do in order to use thought-forms successfully?

CHAPTER 10

YOUR BASIC ATTITUDE

AGAIN I am going to ask you to be patient and not skip over to the details of technique. You have one more important idea to solidify before getting down to the fine points.

That idea that I want to impress on you is this: *Act* daily in full faith that your basic thought-form IS working out. Perhaps that does not sound so terribly important, but let me assure you that it is.

It would be easy here to give you a long list of Don'ts in the use of thought-forms. But instead, for the time being, we shall concentrate on one *big* DO. And we may find that, by inference, it will provide all the Don'ts.

Now read this carefully: The degree of success which you enjoy in using thought-power will correspond exactly with the degree to which your *habitual*, daily attitude toward Life is *constructive*. Why? Because your habitual, daily attitude toward Life reflects your *real underlying* thought-form. If it is constructive your results will be so. And *vice versa*.

By way of example, consider what would happen if a drop of white paint were mixed with a whole tube of black paint. What would you have? *Black* paint, of course. Now suppose a man has a head full of black thoughts. And suppose that by chance he let one little white thought into it. Obviously, his head would still be full of *black* thoughts.

Going still further, if over a period of years a man has poured a stream of black thoughts into the Universal, and then suddenly introduces one little white thought — the Universal remains, *to him*, a sea of black. These black thoughts need not be what we usually call evil ones. They can be just careless ones, or doubtful, or hesitant, or unhappy and distrustful.

Such a man need not expect *one* constructive thought-form at once to undo the harm of millions of destructive thought-forms he has consciously or otherwise impressed on the Universal. Such a man will require perhaps *years* of effort to nullify his previous ignorant actions. This seems like hard lines, in a way—yet we may be sure, on the other hand, that once this has been accomplished, the evil has been put behind FOREVER. Or, as some say, *"our sins have been forgiven."*

Now let us consider the man of good heart, jolly, cheerful and optimistic by nature. His *basic* thought-form of life is constructive and *has been* for years. To him, by contrast with the pessimist, the Universal is white, and even his occasional weak moment will not appreciably discolor it. So to the optimistic man things come easily, but for the pessimistic man life is a burden. You have noticed that yourself, I am sure, speaking by and large.

And here is the scientific, convincing reason for that fact which you have observed: the optimistic, good-expecting man creates good conditions for himself by his daily, inherent thought-forms—unconscious, to be sure, but nevertheless *somewhat* effective. And the pessimistic individual creates his own bad conditions, by a like process.

So we see that so-called Good and Evil are manifestations of exactly the same law, differently applied, but brought about by one and the same power without discrimination. Only in the long run Good prevails over Evil, or evolution would be unthinkable.

Now, if you will analyze the foregoing remarks, you will discover an apparent paradox. We said in one breath that the Universal is *white* to one man, and then we said that to another it is *black.* Yet there can be but one Universal or Infinite. How can it be both black and white?

The answer lies in the fact that while the Universal does not *itself* change, the individual's apperception of it varies all the way from pure white to pure black—or from pure *good* to pure *bad.*

Then are we to say that the Universal is different to different men? My friends, that is *exactly* what we ARE to say. Now let us drop the term "Universal" for the time being, and use a word that means Universal—GOD. Let us try to remain cool and consider this idea on its own merits.

God is different to different men, for MAN CREATES HIS OWN CONCEPTION OF GOD.

One of the most penetrating truths of religion was voiced by an avowed critic of it. You have heard, no doubt, the saying that "an honest man is the noblest work of God." Robert Ingersoll very cleverly, if cynically, reversed that saying, and in doing so, pointed out to mental scientists what really sums up their entire creed. He said: *"An honest God is the noblest work of man."* Think *that* over.

If you have followed these discussions carefully, you must see that in a sense each man does create his own GOD. I say it with all due reverence, for you understand that this means that he decides for himself what God shall *be* to him—or, if you prefer, what the Universal Mind shall do for him.

Do you wonder that theologians for centuries have fought over definitions of God? How could they possibly have agreed among themselves, since they differed in *their own natures* from each other?

However, we need not pause over their disputes. All we need know is that each of us has the almost miraculous power of creating our own individual conception of God. Do we say that He is just—and do we act and speak DAILY as though we believe Him just? Then He IS just. Do we believe that He will supply us with all good things—and do we act DAILY as though we believe that? Then He *does* supply us with all good things. Do we believe that He will answer a constructive thought-form by bringing it to pass — and do we act DAILY as though we believe it? Then He *does* bring it to pass.

That is how simple it is! And that is the meaning of the scriptual warning that "as a man thinketh in his heart, so is he." Not what he *says* he thinks. Not what he thinks occasionally when he *remembers to think it*. But what he thinketh IN HIS HEART —daily, habitually and without reserve. That is what he IS—in the world of thought—and that is what he becomes in the objective world.

The mental scientist who is alive to his task will, curiously enough, exhibit to the world a perfect bevy of the homely virtues. He will be anything but spectacular in his actions, and perhaps seem even stupid to some bright minds because he is not continually scheming to advance his interests.

But how incredibly *superior* is such a mental scientist? That one great lesson he has learned leads him to leave ways and means to the Universal Ways and Means Committee, once he has decided the direction and manner in which that power shall manifest in HIS life.

This does not mean that he sits back and does nothing! Far from it!!! He will be decidedly active in discharging his duties, and doing well the thing at hand. But the greatest Master who has yet appeared to us said, "Take no *anxious* thought for the morrow" and the mental scientist lives strictly by that rule.

Longfellow has well summed up this thought in an immortal stanza in his Psalm of Life:

"Trust no future, howe'er pleasant!
Let the dead Past bury its dead!
Act, act in the living present!
Heart within, and God o'erhead!"

The worker in thought-forms leaves to others all worry as to whether he will get his just reward. He KNOWS that he will. He radiates good cheer and confidence — not because some "pep-up-artist" has told him to, but because he *cannot* be any other way.

He knows that LIFE has a *real meaning*, and he is eager to enter its experiences on the credit side of his ledger. He seeks every opportunity to enlarge the useful sphere of those experiences, both with ideas and with people.

He knows that Love and Beauty walk hand in hand down the by-ways of life, as twin agents of the Universal Mind, and he finds them equally in the song of a lark or the glad cry of a child, in a lump of soft clay or a dancing sunbeam, in the caress of a loved one or the smile of a friend.

Such a person, who has come to AT-ONE-MENT with Universal Mind, and who understands its infinite bounty, truly inhabits a world of the wondrous, "far surpassing wealth unspoken."

Does anyone doubt that such a world is indeed possible? It awaits only the will to find it, to open the door—in short, to use the key which already has been placed *in your hands.*

It requires mainly the formation of your basic thought-form, and then living your life in full confidence that this thought-form is working out in your life. Though you hear countless talks on this subject, and read all the books ever written about it, you will never be closer to the essence of the idea than you are right now.

Many further details need consideration, but that is the vital essence of the idea.

CHAPTER 11

HEALTH AND WEALTH

AND now perhaps it is high time that we get down to cases and discuss some practical examples of how to use thought-forms—and how *not* to use them. Here they are, but please remember that they are only *examples,* and are not suggested specifically for your own use. Everyone should develop his own thought-forms without suggestions from others. But these examples will serve to make certain important points clearer to the novice.

Let us go back to our previous example of how a man sold a house. He listed it with brokers, and then formed a complete picture of that house already sold and himself moving out, etc. *It worked.*

What would have been a wrong way of operating such a thought-form? One of the worst things he could have done would have been to picture a *certain* prospect buying it. That would have violated the rule of not specifying the channel or person, time or method by which the thought-form shall operate.

Or my friend might have formed a picture of himself moving into a new home after leaving the one he had. That would not have been wrong, but it would have been too *indirect,* too *remote.* It is better to confine the thought-form to the immediate desire in hand.

Yet either of these two less desirable thought-forms would have been preferable to none. Most anyone would have tried to sell his house merely by mentioning its availability at every opportunity to friends, by advertising it widely in the newspapers—by *objectively* seeking, in other words, the specific answer to his problem. In one case out of many this method, to be sure, would have worked. But a properly worked out thought-form, if persisted in, will *always* work.

Do not worry if you find it difficult at first to frame your desires completely and simply. Your *real* meaning will be clear to the Universal Mind without lengthy and detailed instructions. But be sure you do have a definite idea yourself. If you find it hard to phrase, it may be that you have not yet as definite a desire as you think you have.

Some students, with all sincerity and the best intentions in the world, begin to concentrate on wealth. Now wealth in itself need not be despised, but wealth sought merely as an end generally destroys the individual who gets it. You have seen that yourself. Wealth does not always accomplish the purpose originally desired.

Many times in the passing years have I heard people say: "Wait till I have made enough money and then I want to devote my entire time to humanitarian work." And I have watched and waited and I have never seen *one* of them acquire what he considered enough to enable him to relax and devote himself to the really useful side of life. Yet many of them have made what the world calls "wealth."

When you concentrate to impress your thought-form upon the Universal, do *not* ask for money or wealth first. *There may be a better way.* Follow the rules given and picturize yourself doing the exact work you desire to do, *regardless of money.* The fact that you become able to do the thing you desire to do is evidence that the means for you to do so will be forthcoming. The best plan for all thought-forms is to see yourself in them doing the actual work you want to do. Then do not "cramp" the Universal by trying to impress it with the idea of just what the desire will cost or when the means shall come or through what channels. What do you care how the supply comes so long as you are doing your work? That is the big thing—the ONLY thing for you to concentrate on.

Study the teachings of the Nazarene Master in the light of what we have been saying, for in them you may find a surprising rest and peace and the assurance of a haven to which all are welcome. They are simple to understand, when read in the true light, but in practicing them we come face to face with ourselves, and discover that human nature is prone to wander from the strict path of constructive and equitable action and thought. Yet this, too, can be overcome.

If and when you find it difficult to follow the precepts of the great laws of nature which are bound to produce harmony, it is because somehow you are thinking wrong. Stop where you are, and wait until your inner guidance tells you that you are back on the clear road to straight and correct thinking, for as your thoughts are, so will the results be, and if you are jangled in your thoughts you will be jangled and confused in your actions and affairs.

Jot this rule down in your memory and, paradoxical as it may seem, *believe* it. If you are as poor as the proverbial church-mouse, never think poverty. If you are as rich as Croesus, never think of yourself as wealthy. But ALWAYS THINK OF YOURSELF AS OPULENT. Many a financially poor man is so rich in courage and stamina that he is bound to rise out of his poverty. Many a rich man is so poor in spirit that his money is the only thing that gets him by, and he frequently loses that. But the *opulent* man, the one who, rich or poor, is conscious of his *fullness* of the good things of life, health, spirit, resilience, the ability to feel himself one with all God's creation, a brother and friend to all and able to feel the beauty of a sunset, the rhythm of a symphony, the language of trees and flowers and animals, will sooner or later enjoy, physically and spiritually, ALL the things this world can shower upon him, simply because he is a part of all good things and by the Law of Attraction they will come to him. He can have "infinite riches in a little room."

Talking and thinking poverty, whether of means or of spirit, creates or perpetuates poverty. Talking or thinking of wealth crystallizes the mind to such an extent that one forgets that riches sometimes take wings, or else develops a spirit of aloofness and arrogance. Talk and think OPULENCE, or having an abundance of the good things of life, including the opportunity to serve others.

Another element in life that most of us worry about at some time or other is health. Good health, since it depends almost entirely on one's own actions, without reference to the thoughts or desires of others, is one of the easiest achievements of the mental scientist.

Remember that the subjective mind is in direct charge of the life processes within you. Its power over assimilation, digestion, excretion, the flow of the blood, nerve force, etc., is unquestioned. Consciously you do not control any of these activities —ordinarily.

But since you now know that you *can* control the subjective mind by your objective mind, then perhaps the most immediate effect you can get with thought-forms is good health, since that depends so directly on the action of the subjective.

In using thought-forms to improve your health, the very first thing is to eliminate the thought of the specific trouble or ailment that you wish to get rid of. Do not picture yourself overcoming a weak heart, for instance, by imagining that weak heart of yours getting stronger.

Whatever your complaint, its cure by thought-form is the same: Concentrate on a picture of yourself WHOLE, HEALTHY, VITAL and STRONG. Imagine yourself doing the things you think you cannot do now. Not impossible things, of course. Just the normal things that healthy people can do.

Remember always that you are a part of and a channel for all the Power in the Universe. That Power will manifest through you in just the degree that YOU permit. Floods of health and strength are waiting for you, and will flow to you when you have built a thought-form of yourself of a constructive nature as to health.

So first banish any idea that you are sick. Yes— you may be, but do not dwell on it. We do not suggest that you deny your illness, if you have one, for that would be absurd. There is no point in avoiding a fact; it is better to eliminate an unpleasant fact. We are not advocating metaphysical quibblings, but simply pointing out how to overcome unpleasant physical facts without stultifying your reason by affirming their non-existence.

Having eliminated, or at least subdued, the consciousness of your pain or illness, meditate at length on yourself as glowing with health. See the results of that state: yourself full of "pep," active, alert, able to keep going a long time without being over-tired, etc.

Then concentrate that picture into a thought-form and stamp it, as you have been directed, on the Universal Mind. If you are too thin, visualize yourself gaining weight, and healthily so. If you are too fat, see yourself thinner—not to the exclusion of any other aspect of good health, but merely as one part of the picture.

Even medical science concedes the value of the state of mind in maintaining good health. Today good doctors use less medicine and more "psychology," by calling upon the sick person's mentalism and "will-to-health." What a doctor can do along those lines for you, you can do directly for yourself, although this is not to deny the value of proper medicine or surgery for acute conditions.

Invisible potencies of all kinds are now in every-day use for good health, and the greatest of these is the power of mind rightly directed.

85

CHAPTER 12

EMPLOYMENT

THESE days a job or the absence of it seems to be uppermost in the minds of many people. How can you get a job—or a better one—by using a thought-form?

Not so long ago a man I know was out of a job. He knew about thought-forms, but—having had an easy life up to then—had not bothered to use them. After several months of idleness, with his funds disappearing rapidly, he suddenly woke up to the fact that he was merely doing what everyone else was doing who was out of work—walking from place to place wherever he hoped there might be a job, and advertising in the newspapers. And he was rapidly getting nowhere.

He decided that he would "come to life" and use the power of thought-forms. But *how*, was the question?

There was a certain office where he felt sure he could be useful. He had once worked there, could do certain things for that organization, and believed that he might, without loss to anyone, well be employed there.

So he set up a picture of himself at work there, right in the office and at a certain desk he knew was not then being used. He clearly outlined the kind of papers he would be working on. He visualized himself receiving a pay envelope. He built up many details of the picture, and then impressed it hard and often on the Universal Mind.

He got the job.

Was that a successful thought-form? Apparently so, for he got what he was after. But he failed in one important point, and soon afterwards lost the job! What was the thing he did wrong, and which therefore brought him only temporary and mild success with that thought-form? Do you see it?

His mistake was in specifying the *particular* office he was to be employed at. He believed they needed him, and the power of his thought created a temporary condition that agreed with his idea. But basically he was wrong—they did *not* need him, and his thought-form could not permanently overcome that fact.

What should he have done? Just what he did, except that he should not have specified the office. He should first have meditated fully on the manner in which his talents could well be used by *somebody* —not a specific person. He should have pictured himself in *an* office doing the kind of work he wanted, as part of a chain of effort that was giving his community a real service of some kind—and receiving a pay envelope.

What is really the essence of employment? Is it not *service?* That is a much-abused word these days, but it is an honorable one, nevertheless. If you desire—honestly and completely—to be *useful,* and impress that idea on the Universal Mind, the way will be found. The answer may be entirely different from what you expect, but, when it comes, accept it whole-heartedly and put all of yourself into whatever it suggests.

The story about the man which I have just related — a true one, by the way — has a happy ending. After being discharged from the job he secured, he had wit enough to realize his error. He went right to work on another thought-form of a more general nature, without specifications as to how or where it would work out. His emphasis was put on himself as really serving. A close friend of his soon came to him and hired him for a totally unexpected kind of work, which he was glad to undertake, and that job he has held, with his pay increased twice since.

I cannot tell you the exact nature of the thought-form you should set up to get yourself a job. I can and have told you what to do in a general way — which is all anyone *can* tell you.

Now let me add a few Don'ts.

Do not see yourself *replacing* anyone in a job. That would probably be bad for the other person, and so could not do you good.

Do not specify minutely the kind of work you want to do. *There may be a better kind of work for you.*

Do not say that you are going to get a job *by such a time.* Your best work may not be ready for you, and no matter what your present needs may be, your best work will be better for you in the long run if you have the courage to wait for it!

Do not see yourself getting money by clever deals with other people. Those clever deals may not be good for the others, so they will not be good for you.

Do not see yourself hoarding the results of your labors. There is plenty for All—even though few know it. There is certainly plenty for you. See yourself *using* the fruits of your labors constructively—to help others, to serve the community, to build up the business you become a part of.

These are a few of the principal errors to be avoided. There are others that you will find for yourself unless you stay close to the general rules laid down. And above all, remember that after you have made up your thought-form correctly, and consistently stamped it on the Universal Mind, you must act in full confidence that it *has* become a fact in the world of thought, and *will* come true before your very eyes.

CHAPTER 13

HOW TO CONCENTRATE

IN THE technique of forming mental pictures we must emphasize the importance of *concentration*, a principle about which many people talk and write—but which few know how to put into actual practice. It is easy to form a mental picture. Every one has done so and continues to do so to a greater or lesser extent. Day dreams are such pictures. Even the most "unimaginative" person forms pictures in his mind of the desires or longings closest to his heart.

Ideas MUST express themselves, and in order to become full fledged ideas they *must* picturize themselves in one's consciousness. If you propose to build a house, you may be hazy about details but you have SOME IDEA of about how you expect it to look, and you try to convey your general mental picture to your architect, leaving the detailed drawings and specifications to him, if you are wise.

In forming thought-forms you are commending your ideas to the Great Architect of the Universe.

The more you retain your pictured idea in your mind, seldom letting it out of your consciousness, even though you may be engaged on other matters, the stronger that picture becomes. It grows by its own nature, for growth is a cosmic law that applies to things on the mental plane as well as on the physical.

We keep our mental picture or thought-form in continuous, healthy growth by the process and faculty of *concentration.* An eastern philosopher, Patanjali, defines concentration as "the hindering of the modifications of the thinking principle." In plainer words, it means the prevention of thoughts that interfere with any important matter on which we have set our minds. It means devoting one's unhindered mental energies to the particular matter that stands out in importance above all other things in our life at any one time.

Concentration means being of "one mind" for the period in which you are holding your thought-form for impression upon the Universal Mind. There must be no confusion. You cannot develop your thought-form and impress it upon the Universal and at the same time allow side thoughts to flit across your mental vision. Devolpment of concentration is natural to some, difficult for others: but any normal person CAN develop it by simple perseverance.

If, at the start, your mind wanders, bring it back to focus again and again until your picture remains clear and unobscured. Again, if your mind persists in wandering, in spite of all your efforts, it shows that what you *think* you desire does not take the precedence it should and that it is not, for the moment, the all-absorbing interest in your life. To be successful, it MUST be the all-absorbing interest, to the exclusion of all else at that time. This does not mean that you must think of nothing else at any time. Go about your ordinary affairs, but with the knowledge that the thought-form upon which you are working is very close beneath your surface consciousness and can be brought up to focus at any moment. Have an underlying consciousness of your supreme desire, and as many times as possible each day bring it to focus and impress it again and again upon the Universal Mind.

In concentrating upon your thought-form, hold it steady, clear and fixed. But there is another way in which you can help. *Meditate* upon it. Meditation is somewhat like concentration but not the same. In concentration the thought or picture is held fixed. In meditation the general idea is held, but one allows the mind to revolve the idea in every direction, developing its possibilities, and then adding such developments to the fixed idea. Meditate *first* to build up a fine thought-form. Then contemplate calmly and expectantly its working out.

Now notice carefully that it is *not* by concentration or meditation that you consciously create circumstances. It is *only* by impressing your thought-forms on the subjective and visualizing them worked out that you bring them about. Concentration and meditation are needed to help you do this stamping. Your WILL holds the thought constant to its purpose — but the thought alone CREATES.

Probably you have seen a steel die or copper plate from which stationery is engraved. The surface of the metal is hollowed out in the form of the monogram to be printed. As a die alone it is practically worthless. Yet when the ink is put into it, and transferred under pressure to the paper, the finished product is useful.

Conceive of your thought-form as the die. When the proper materials come to hand, the die or thought-form impresses your life with events as determined by its own form. The common expression, "The die is cast" takes on greater significance in this connection.

Sometimes concentration is taught by having the student fix his attention outwardly on some physical object, like a glass of water, or a point within a circle. While this may be of value, resort to mechanical means is unnecessary, and the resulting phenomena are not in the long run as constructive as direct training of the mind, *by* the mind, *in* the mind.

The sort of concentrative ability you need must

be the vigorous, active kind that will operate any-
where and under any conditions without an external stimulus. In seeking this, first relax. Close
the eyes. Take a comfortable posture. In other
words, *remove* external distractions. Allow your
mind to calm down. Then—

DEVELOP THE PICTURE OF YOUR DESIRE. Fill in
as many details as you can without specifying how
they shall come about. Gradually, like a photo-
graphic film developing, the picture will take on
more and more meaning, until it suddenly jumps
into completion. Then FIX IT. Hold on to it for a
few minutes. Then banish it and forget it. Relax.

Later on, recall the picture to your mind. Repeat
this process often. There is no such thing as too
much concentration, unless you do so much of it
at any one time that you become over-tired.

Remember that the Universal Mind is constructive. Yet because Universal Mind is impersonal, it
has no choice but to follow the plan laid down in
the charge, mission or burden that is given it by
you. Therefore it will work for you, and on returning your plan or thought-form completed and in
objective manifestation, it will involve you just
as you wanted to be involved. If, therefore, your
thought-form has in it any element of personal
grievance or harm for another, it will come back
to you and you will still be involved, which is just

what you do NOT want. So make sure that your plans are right and worthy, for be it week, month, year or centuries, the bread cast on the waters will return.

Sometimes the question is asked: "Can I function more than one thought-form at a time?" The answer is that only one thought-form can be impressed upon the Universal Mind at one "stamping." But having with deep concentration impressed the Universal Mind with a fundamental thought-form, there is nothing to prevent you from making other impresses upon the Universal Mind for other purposes. The real test is whether you can focus your objective mind on more than one purpose without weakening the varied purposes you have in mind. Sometimes a person may have several desires which, when properly put into definite shape, indicate that one single, well-expressed thought-form will furnish the basic essentials to cover all those desires.

If it is desired to develop two thought-forms and to impress them upon the Universal Mind, the individual must make sure that his mind is entirely clear of the one while he devotes it to the other. Otherwise "confusion in the craft" will result. It is better to set one well-defined thought-form into activity and wait until it is firmly started on the way to externalization, and then later impress the second thought-form as a distinct entity by itself.

Take the first steps slowly. Ponder your objectives carefully. Then work hard on one basic thought-form before you clutter up your mental workshop with a lot of half-built, weak structures.

CHAPTER 14

FEAR AND FAITH

SOME people feel that they understand the law perfectly as soon as their attention has been directed to it. They begin to practice it and as soon as they begin, they also begin to nullify it by their doubts. It seems so simple at first that they begin to question: "How is it possible to secure what I need merely by closing my eyes and speaking to myself?" That is one question that arises. "I wonder if it is true; if it will work out for me just as I have been taught?" is another. And so on.

When an individual begins to wonder, or question a thought-form's power in any way, he has only one thing to do, and that is to begin all over again, for he has sent out thoughts that have weakened or destroyed his brain children almost the moment they were born.

These mental states of wonderment, hope, questioning and similar conditons all evidence an inner fundamental doubt, and doubt is fatal to success in any phase of activity. Doubt is a mild form of expressing something stronger and more dangerous —FEAR OF FAILURE. "Our doubts," as Shakespeare has it, "are traitors, and make us lose the good we oft might win, by fearing to attempt."

Maybe you are familiar with the following story, but in any event, it is apropos.

A traveler met the Black Plague on the way to Bagdad. "Where are you going?" asked the traveler. "To Bagdad, to slay five thousand," said the Plague.

Later on, the traveler met the Plague returning, and said to it:

"You told me you were going to kill only five thousand, but I hear that fifty thousand died." "I told you truly," said the Plague. "I slew only five thousand, the other forty-five thousand *were killed through fear.*"

Closer to our own times is the case of the preacher in North Carolina who allowed himself to be bitten by a rattlesnake, which is ordinarily fatal unless immediately treated. He recovered. He would have no physician. He said (according to *The New York Times*): "Not for a moment have I lost my faith. I had faith in the Lord that He would take care of me." And this preacher's sublime faith drew from the eminent scientist Dr. Ditmars, according to credible press reports, the astounding statement: "I do not advise preachers or any one else to follow the example this mountain man has set, but I will say that I respect this particular preacher's faith. I believe his faith and his general health will pull him through. Faith AND THE STATE OF MIND, I believe, have a good deal to do with a man's physical condition, and this man's religion has buoyed him up mentally."

Fear must be conquered before you can reasonably expect to attain real success in *anything*, and the conquest of fear may be one of the very best things you can ask first from the Universal Mind. All doubts MUST be eliminated, and you can start to accomplish this by forming a mental picture of yourself doing courageously and positively just the thing you are most fearful of. It will be a self-discipline that will stand you in good stead for the rest of your lifetime.

Many failures in this world, where the individual is apparently gifted with every working tool that destiny can furnish him, arise from this deep, inner *fearfulness*, fear of criticism, fear of ridicule, fear of competition, fear of superior power, education, place, financial status. All these produce an inferiority complex that breaks down many a useful man or woman.

There is an old scriptural saying that "No man liveth unto himself." That this is true will be seen on a moment's reflection. When you impress your thought-form upon the Universal Mind, you must remember that because the Universal Mind is universal it operates through *all* human individual minds. Therefore, your thought-form is going to make a definite impression upon others. More than this, the fact that your thought-form is going to be impressed upon other individual minds, and that they are going to react to it according to their capacities for reception, shows us that we do not live unto ourselves alone, but impress ourselves most potently upon others for good or ill. It behooves us to make sure that it IS for good and NOT for ill. This impression is made upon others through their subjective minds, and will manifest according to the measure by which their subjective minds can react upon their objective mentalism. It shows the underlying unity that is the basic principle of the real concept of human brotherhood.

So it is emphasized all through the subject of mental science that you must make your thought-forms constructive. Note well—not that such are the *only* kind that will ever work. But that constructive thought-forms are the only kind that will SURELY WORK to your ultimate advantage every time. And that is the only kind you are interested in.

Do we by chance need any further *proof* that these principles are *true?* The testimony of many of our greatest souls agrees with us.

Let us turn to the Great Book, where we find: "All things whatsoever ye shall ask in prayer, *believing,* ye shall receive." (Matt. 21:22) The only stipulation is that the seeker must BELIEVE that he shall receive what he seeks. "Whatsoever ye shall ask *in my name*, that will I do." Note—*"in my name"*— in other words, *constructively.* And again, "If ye shall ask anything in my name, I will do it." (John 14:13, 14.)

Is it not notable that we are told to ASK not once but *many times* throughout the Scriptures? The admonition or privilege is not an obscure text, but one that is reiterated throughout the Christian teaching.

Prior to Christianity, Buddha emphasized the same principles. He said: "Good thoughts will produce good actions, and bad thoughts will produce bad actions. Hatred does not cease by hatred at any time; hatred ceases by love; this is an old rule." Here is the direct substantiation of the teaching that worthy thought-forms tend to constructive actions and results. Also that revengeful thought-forms work only a continuation of the wrong mental attitude. The thought-form that does not embody love of one's fellow beings has no right to externalization.

The knowledge of the wide difference in the application of the objective mind as applying to outer things and the subjective as applying to the inner is shown by Lao Tze, the Chinese philosopher. Said he: "The Sage attends to the inner and not to the outer." In other words, as we say, he puts aside the objective and holds to the subjective when really important things are to be undertaken.

As we might expect from his mathematical mode of expression, Pythagoras gives the law we have explained in the lines from his famous Golden Verses:

> "For a most rigid law
> Binds Power to Necessity."

Or, as we would put it, the whole Power of Universal Mind is at the disposal of Man's Necessity. There must therefore be a direct way in which it can be invoked, also by which it can react. Thought-forms are the way.

It is useless for anyone to undertake the practice of developing and impressing thought-forms merely from the standpoint of experiment, or to "see if the thing will work." He must enter upon such an important undertaking only after he has satisfied himself completely that the law is logical, natural, practical and excellent. Only a supreme confidence in one's relationship to the Universal Mind will beget results. Neither is the Universal Source of all Supply amenable to the "gimme" kind of prayers wherein the one who so prays is under the delusion that it is far more blessed to receive than to give. All requests made upon the Universal should be formulated from the standpoint of becoming an instrument through which the Universal can work in greater freedom of expression to reach the greatest number for good.

Do not get the idea that you are using something new and untried. The law of supply through impressing the Universal Mind with your particular needs has been known for ages, but the vast majority of mankind has lost sight of it in their haste to secure their ends through what they consider visible, tangible means, relying in false pride upon what they call "their own ability." Well, our ability, so-called, is simply the measure by which we utilize the vast power within us, whether we do so consciously or unconsciously.

John Burroughs, whose life was an undoubted success and whose fine qualities made an immortal impress upon human consciousness, sums up the attitude required of the novice who seeks success through individual at-one-ment with the Universal Mind. He says:

> "Serene I fold my hands and wait,
>   Nor care for wind, nor tide, nor sea;
> I rave no more 'gainst time or fate,
>   For lo, my own shall come to me."

In these beautiful lines we find no attempt at limitation. The Universal is not urged to produce results at a given time or place. There is no worry, anxiety or mental distress. Instead, in the next verse, we find his full acquiescence with whatsoever his environment imposes upon him. He says:

103

"I stay my haste, I make delays;
   For what avails this eager pace?
I stand amid the eternal ways,
   And what is mine, shall know my face."

And then, as though there were some deep, inner diapason of victory, a sustaining sense of triumph over all earthly barriers, the poet sends out upon the ethers to a posterity that shall listen with reverence in years to come, these inspired lines that attain to sheer grandeur:

"The stars come nightly to the sky;
   The tidal wave comes to the sea;
Nor time, nor space, nor deep, nor high,
   Can keep my own away from me."

CHAPTER 15

THE SPIRIT OF YOUR THOUGHT

WE have now covered most points about thought-forms that you need to know to use them with some degree of success for yourself. If you like, you need go no further in our discussions, but use merely what has already been given. It will work for you.

But you *can* do more. You can *make it work for others,* as well. And if you *do* use this marvelous power to help others, that in turn will help you.

In using thought-forms to help others, follow the rules already given, but substitute the other person in place of yourself. In the matter of health, visualize the other person well, happy, strong, vital. If employment is the objective, see the other person busy at a useful task, earning money. And so on. The principle is the same.

But be very, very sure when you use a thought-form for another that it is to his or her advantage. What you *think* would be good for another might not be good at all. Hesitate always before taking action on the mental plane for another (as well as for yourself), for in working a thought-form for another you are involving yourself in the results of it, and you may not like them if things do not work out as you think they should, through your imperfect use of the idea.

One safe way to help another—and in my opinion the very best way—is to HELP HIM TO HELP HIMSELF, for then he puts his own efforts into the work and the results will mean more. This applies to thought-forms in particular. You may even go so far as to talk to the person who needs help, *about* thought-forms, so that he can use them for himself, if he is open-minded enough to concede the possibility of their value.

We need not seek to solve all the world's problems, but we will do well to help another person in some way when the chance comes our way. Such an action gives an outlet through us to the constructive activity of Universal Mind, for wherever Universal Mind IS—and that is everywhere—there we also find it seeking an opportunity to help its own creatures.

Wherever the Universal Mind IS, there also we find love—love for its own creatures like the love of a parent for his children — only on a grander scale, and never failing. And love in a human being "is ever the beginning of knowledge, as fire is of light."

Love and Life are inseparable. Sometime we may discover that they are one and the same Principle, in creative and ethical polarities. Life being everywhere, creation is therefore still going on everywhere. Your thoughts, reaching out into this ocean of creative activity, can direct its energies to your purposes, and if those purposes are in alignment with the nature and intent of the First Creative Purpose, and if they betoken Progress for All, your desires will be more speedily realized.

This is the essence of the admonition to become "chosen vessels of the Lord." To become or to make one's self a chosen vessel implies a direct personal responsibility, one that we have not generally observed to be stressed by most self-help philosophies of the day, which are devoted mainly to the general subject of "How to get what YOU want." The correlative responsibility is TO USE WHAT YOU GET. It seems to be a law of Nature that only use brings out or keeps up what we have. If we do not use our brains, they do not develop. If we do not use our muscles, they atrophy. If we do not use our house, it deteriorates; the roof begins to leak, pipes go bad, window panes are broken and the house assumes a general appearance of decrepitude. If we have wealth and do not use it for the common good, we either become useless misers or someone takes it from us. If we have talents and do not use them profitably, they diminish or are taken away.

There is law back of all this. Forces in nature are in a state of constant flux—ebb and flow. The stream goes on continuously, with waves of action and re-action. If we keep on with our course, we ride the waves. If we drift, we move around in circles with the counter waves, and get nowhere. If we have talents and put them into use, they multiply and one result leads to another still more worth while. If we have means we must keep them in circulation, casting the bread upon the waters that it may come back to us after many days. The one who hoards talent, ability, wealth, energy, finds that in due time it becomes a menace to him. YOU CAN ONLY KEEP BY GIVING AWAY, paradoxical as that may seem.

Some years ago, a wealthy New Yorker bought a large tract of land in the Adirondacks. Streams ran through it and watered adjacent lands and every one was happy and prosperous. But the new landowner wanted the streams for himself. He built dams, so that he could enjoy artificial falls and a small lake. In due time the lake became larger, but the water, shut off from its natural course, no longer nourished the adjacent lands and they suffered; vegetation dwindled to nothing and poverty existed where before there had been plenty. The rich man's lake grew still larger and in time it flooded his own lands and spoiled what had been a place of beauty. Marshes formed. Stagnant pools developed. Mosquitoes found it a delightful summer resort. The stubborn man only felt that he had been cheated and refused to do a thing.

Finally, the farmers adjacent to him took the law into their own hands, broke down the dams, let the water back on its natural course, and in due time order was restored, but only after hatred, revenge and suffering had been engendered. To this day, the wealthy owner will not go up there; neither will he sell his land. Meantime, the others who do live there are happy again. Moral, the foolish one by his selfish refusal to put himself in alignment with the natural forces, has crowded himself out of what might have been a little Paradise.

The example just cited is by way of illustrating the responsibility that possession of anything entails, whether it be wealth, talent, brains or ability.

Do not formulate a thought-form of anything unless you have a deep, intensive interest in *using it*. For instance, it would be of no use for you to wish for wealth solely that you might *escape work*. Wealth brings definite responsibilities. Are you as anxious to *assume them,* apply them, USE them? If not, think up a better thought-form! You cannot use Universal Mind to evade work, responsibility, or to look forward to a life of laziness, uselessness or idleness. The wise bees and ants do not permit that, and neither will Nature permit it in the human species without payment of some kind, which may not be pleasant to him who pays. That we have some such idlers at the moment is merely the result of accumulated motion, wherein we have not yet learned how to distribute the profusion of wealth of many kinds that an overgenerous Nature so lavishly bestows.

Truly, anything that is right, constructive and worthy, IS within the reach of any intelligent human being, if that being will only set himself in alignment with the forces whose assistance he seeks. When you have formulated your thought-form, by impressing it upon the Universal Mind you create a *mental prototype*. It is actually accomplished. That is why you HAVE received, even before you see it in manifestation. This prototype grows, by the law of growth, according to the intensity and frequency with which you "pray without ceasing," i.e., fix it deeper and deeper into the Universal matrix. As it grows, it attracts to itself just the material its complete expression calls for until finally it comes into externalization.

The at-one-ment to be effected by tuning the individual mind to the Universal Mind through a conscious and whole-souled acceptance of its existence, its power, its impersonalness which means no favoritism but equal opportunity to all alike, is well expressed by the Prophet Zachariah: "Not by might, nor by power, BUT BY MY SPIRIT." Therefore, it is most essential (for best results) that we approach Universal Mind from the spiritual point of view as well as the purely mental. In this approach we must keep in mind the requirement set before us by the Nazarene Master, who said, in his own prayers, "Nevertheless, not my will but thine be done." Failure to recognize this principle is one strong reason why some fail who attempt to practice mental science, for "to live by one man's will became the cause of all men's misery," as Richard Hooker wrote over three hundred years ago.

This principle — not my will but *thine* — is the pivotal point around which the well-ordered life of the individual with balanced judgment revolves. It is the properly spiritual attitude. It does not mean passivity. It does not mean sitting around waiting for a Higher Will to make itself manifest. It does mean going to work with all the power we possess and DOING SOMETHING, instead of lolling around and rationalizing our laziness with every kind of sophistry.

By going about it in the right way, ready always to conform his individual will with that of the Universal Will, so to speak, one can effect such a reapprochement with the Universal as to be able to enter into its creative activities and direct those activities to an individual measure of realization. This is what Judge Troward, a great mental scientist, meant when he described this process as one wherein the "Cosmic Intelligence becomes individualized and the individual intelligence becomes universalized. The two become one."

So I urge you to use thought-forms in this spirit —IF YOU USE THEM AT ALL. Yes, they will work even if you use them for some entirely worthy *personal* motive. But they will work with much greater power if you seek to conform them to Universal Motives, so far as you feel you understand them.

Let your thought-forms—for greatest usefulness to others and therefore to yourself—have back of them a conscious love of Man and God. Whatever your purpose, let it serve also the purpose of the power that has brought you to the point where you are permitted to use thought-forms. In other words, *provide for the equity*—Universal Mind is going to do a lot for you: what are you going to do to serve the purposes of Universal Mind?

Epictetus advises us to dare to look up to God and say, "Make use of me for the future as Thou wilt. I am of the same mind; I am one with Thee. I refuse nothing which seems good to Thee. Lead me whither Thou wilt. Clothe me in whatever dress Thou wilt."

The mental scientist will do well to keep that admonition in mind, and to the degree that he acts and lives it will his life prosper.